Does God Forgive Me?

AUGUST GOLD, author of *Where Does God Live?*

Photo illustrations by DIANE HARDY WALLER

Walking Together, Finding the Way

SKYLIGHT PATHS®
PUBLISHING
Woodstock, Vermont

Does God Forgive Me?
2006 First Printing
Text © 2006 by August Gold
Photos © 2006 by Diane Hardy Waller

For information regarding permission to reprint material from this book, please mail or fax your request in writing to SkyLight Paths Publishing, Permissions Department, at the address / fax number listed below, or e-mail your request to permissions@skylightpaths.com.

Library of Congress Cataloging-in-Publication Data
Gold, August, 1955–
Does God forgive me? / August Gold ; photo illustrations by Diane Hardy Waller.
      p. cm.
ISBN 1-59473-142-X
1. Forgiveness of sin—Juvenile literature. 2. Forgiveness—Religious aspects—Christianity—Juvenile literature. I. Waller, Diane Hardy. II. Title.

BT795.G65 2006
234'.5—dc22

2005031359

10 9 8 7 6 5 4 3 2 1

Manufactured in Hong Kong
Cover design & interior typesetting: Jenny Buono

Grateful acknowledgment is given for permission to print the following photographs: p. 5 © Rebecca Ellis, p. 7 © Greg Nicholas, p. 16 © Jamie Wilson, p. 26 © Charity Myers, p. 31 © Renee Lee, all reprinted courtesy of www.istockphoto.com; p. 15 © Rosanne Saltzman; p. 18 © Pat Curry Gore.

SkyLight Paths Publishing is creating a place where people of different spiritual traditions come together for challenge and inspiration, a place where we can help each other understand the mystery that lies at the heart of our existence.

SkyLight Paths sees both believers and seekers as a community that increasingly transcends traditional boundaries of religion and denomination—people wanting to learn from each other, walking together, finding the way.

SkyLight Paths, "Walking Together, Finding the Way," and colophon are trademarks of LongHill Partners, Inc., registered in the U.S. Patent and Trademark Office.

Walking Together, Finding the Way
Published by SkyLight Paths Publishing
A Division of LongHill Partners, Inc.
Sunset Farm Offices, Route 4, P.O. Box 237
Woodstock, VT 05091
Tel: (802) 457-4000   Fax: (802) 457-4004
www.skylightpaths.com

You acted so badly
on Saturday night.
You yelled at your sister
and then picked a fight.

You wouldn't eat dinner,
you threw down your plate,
complaining and whining
about the food you ate.

When Mom told you "No,"
you yelled back, "Yes!"
then proceeded to make
an even bigger mess.

You threw such a tantrum
and kicked toys to the floor.
"I hate you!"
you screamed,
and stormed out the door.

Back in your bedroom,
you cried out your pain
                    'til your pillow was wet
        and completely tear-stained.

Mom and Dad knocked lightly
before entering your room,
                    hugging you tightly
          not a moment too soon.

"Dad, will you punish me for making you MAD?

Can you and Mom forgive me for being so bad?"

"When you do harm, sweetheart,
there is a price to pay.
So sincerely apologize
for what you did today."

"I'm sorry, Mom and Dad,
            and I'll apologize to Sis.
   What I did was **wrong**.
Please FORGIVE me for this!"

"Parents don't expect
a perfect boy or perfect girl.

Even parents make mistakes
in this very human world."

"Does God get ANGRY, too, when I do a mean thing?

Will God's arms stay open and be WELCOMING?"

"No matter what you say
             or what you ever do,
God's loving heart
             NEVER closes to you."

"Mom, are you kidding?
God **loves** me when I'm bad?

When I make trouble
even Daddy gets **MAD!**"

"God's love does not punish,
God's love doesn't blame.
No matter what you do, my dear,
God loves you just the same."

"And if something I say
hurts one of my friends?"

"Then God gives you new words
that help to heal and mend."

"And if my mistakes pile up to the SKY?"

"Then God helps you correct them so they don't multiply."

"What if I take something
 that isn't really mine?"

"Return it and God forgives you
 a thousand, thousand times."

"Then face who you harmed
and do not be ashamed
to make your amends
asking forgiveness in God's name."

"So God's forgiveness is forever
no ifs or ands or buts!
God forgives every one of us
no matter why or when or what!"

"Wow, God's heart must be GiGantic for God's LOVE to be so big—

God LOVES us all FOREVER for as long as we live!"